Howie Schneider
Unshucked

Howie Schneider Unshucked

A Cartoon Collection
about the Cape, the Country
and Life Itself

From the Award-Winning
Feature in the

PROVINCETOWN
BANNER

On
Cape Publications

Yarmouth Port, Massachusetts

10 9 8 7 6 5 4 3 2 1

Printed in Canada.

ISBN: 0-9653283-9-2

For further information:
On Cape Publications
P.O. Box 218, Yarmouth Port, MA 02675

Dedicated to the memory of Mischa Richter,
who knew better than anyone
what it was all about.

And to Susie,
who also sees the bad ones.

Preface

This book contains some of the best of "Howie Schneider Unshucked" from the editorial pages of the *Provincetown Banner*. Howie has been part of the Banner's tradition and mission since our first issue more than six years ago.

It's a tradition that started back in June 1856, with the very first *Provincetown Banner*, which set forth that it would "aim to be tolerant... outspoken and fearless in its advocacy of human liberty." By 1861, the Banner's motto was "Be Just and Fear Not," and it is our motto still. Today's *Provincetown Banner*, whose first issue appeared in May of 1995, carries forward that same spirit of tolerance and honesty, to "be just and fear not" as a community newspaper serving this special curl of land.

And that, as you will see in the pages of this book, is where Howie Schneider's editorial cartoons come in.

It has been our great, good fortune to have "Howie Schneider Unshucked" on our editorial page each week. We can count on his trenchant, wry wit to tug at our peccadilloes and put wayward hubris in its proper place, to hold up a mirror to our follies honestly, justly and fearlessly. Every week we wait for his next salvo – which is unfailingly greeted with a wry smile, a chuckle or a good old-fashioned belly laugh.

We are proud of Howie, proud that his cartoons appear in the *Banner* and proud that they are being published in book form. It is high time, and undoubtedly the toughest job had to be deciding which ones to include. We all have our favorites, and many of them are right here. We hope you enjoy revisiting some of yours, maybe even finding some you missed.

They'll still give you a jab in the ribs with a wink of the eye.

Alix Ritchie
Publisher, *The Provincetown Banner*
and *The Advocate*
on behalf of the entire staff

Foreword

When I was approached by the Banner to do this feature my first reaction was negative. I didn't want to do a local editorial cartoon about zoning issues and political disputes, like the cartoons found in so many weekly newspapers. I was also concerned there wouldn't be enough "real" material to work with.

I was wrong. This is a truly remarkable place with a vibrant mix of people, most of them from other places. Our community problems reflect those of the nation and beyond, and daily life here is an endless source of inspiration.

My career has been devoted almost entirely to comic strips, magazines and books. With all of these there is a considerable time lapse, sometimes months, between the doing and the laughing. A weekly cartoon draws an immediate response. I can hear the laughter and I love it. I consider it a great privilege to live here and contribute whatever it is that cartooning adds to an increasingly baffling world.

Howie Schneider

"I just use him for reading."

"Hey, Pop... can I borrow the earring tonight?"

"I said no pictures!"

"I admit it's going to cost a few bucks but just think of it, folks... the 'North Truro Yankees'."

"Hold it, guys. I think we got a wetland here."

"They fouled the wetlands, polluted the air,
contaminated the water... so what's the big
deal about a little poisoned food?"

"The rents are so high now I found it's
cheaper to take a cab for a month."

"Uh, oh!"

"Your daughter's pregnant, your son got busted,
I wrecked the car and we're out of coffee...
details at six."

23

"He downloaded his first word yesterday."

"...and this was his last painting before
he went mad, poor man."

"Twice a day they fill it with water and the beach disappears.
Who knows why? Where y'from, Cleveland?"

"Looks like it's gonna be a rough day."

"My wife doesn't understand me."

"Oh, wow!... I almost forgot it's Halloween."

*"I've called this meeting to discuss a major development
in our fund drive for the new library."*

"Personally, I think putting a handicap ramp in the monument
was a real dumb idea to begin with."

34

"Talk about a dull winter."

"Do you have any from victim to perpetrator?"

"Actually, Senator... the incident you're referring to when I allegedly relieved myself against the side of the Executive Office building occurred during a break in a very intense campaign day when my needs were correctly perceived as being subservient to the candidate's..."

*"It's one of the finest examples of an old, traditional structure
...and yet it's in full compliance with all the latest regulations."*

"Now remember, summer is almost here. Your mission is to get in there, spread out, take the parking spots, clog up the facilities, spend as little money as possible, take your pictures and get out."

"Grandma! How cool you look."

"Move the question!"

*"We've done all we can for you, Mr. Folsom. It's
now in the hands of the Almighty. And they
don't meet again until next month."*

"After we knock out the Fish and Wildlife Service I promised
Phyllis I'd bring her back a few hundred
of those plover eggs."

"You knucklehead! That's not what I meant by 'take the dog out'!"

"Just let me do the talking, okay?"

*"Again you're going out? Can't you find something
to paint at home once in a while?"*

"I think beach erosion has met its match in Harry Lancaster."

"He could really be great if he ever gets off his ass."

*"It's been a really great season but
I'll be glad when it's over."*

"Poor bastards miss the fleet as much as we do."

"I always knew he was a fair-weather friend."

*"Keep breathing Mrs. Gottbaum. I have a call
in to the rescue squad."*

"And another thing, Madame Moderator..."

*"I'm glad we decided to stay home tonight. I
hate going out New Year's Eve."*

"Your middle name is Harvey? My son's name is Harvey. Named after his grandfather. He's an accountant in New Jersey. Didn't want to follow in his dad's footsteps. Said he wanted to do something more exciting. He got that right. Get's pretty lonely around here. 'Specially this time of the year. How about you? You got kids?"

"I can't break it up. It's a set."

"I hate Memorial Day, man. Ya can't even
find a decent place to take a leak."

"Thank you, sir. Have a nice half hour."

"...and they call this 'on the water'?"

"...and for our specials tonight we have a six-thousand calorie dinner, three eight-thousand calorie dinners and our special twelve-thousand calorie festival blow-out."

"He always had trouble with women."

ABSOLUT GALILEO

"...so the first little pig said, 'I'm gonna build my house with a cesspool,' and the second little pig said, 'I'm gonna build MY house around a great big Title V leaching pit' ...but the third pig said, 'I'm gonna hook MY house up to the sewer system'..."

"I say impeach the son-of-a-bitch. He made us the laughing stock of the whole damn world."

the UNAUTHORIZED PORTRAIT

"The only damn thing not legal out there these days is fishin'."

"My God... It's the Zoning Board of Appeals."

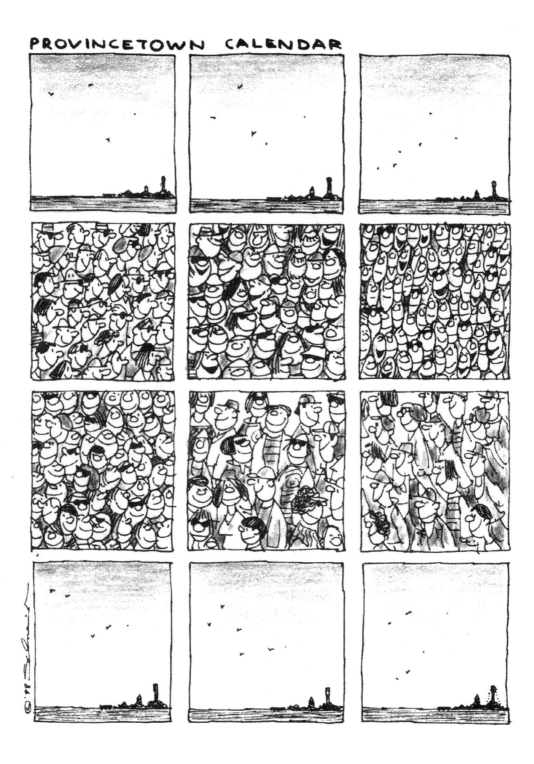

"...then, as alleged, in Document 492, section 12, paragraph B, delivered in hand by the honorable Chairman of the duly appointed Judicial Committee of the honorable House of Representatives to this duly elected Senate of the Congress of the United States of America, an employee of the Executive branch of this government, heretofore referred to as "the Intern," within the confines of the working premises of the Government of the People of the United States of America, did perform upon the duly elected sitting President of these United States of America, in the vernacular of said aforementioned document, a blow-job."

79

"...hearts are in the meat section... courage I believe you'll find in the pharmacy... and brains, if we have any left, would be in the deli."

"...then when my dad wanted to know what the hell I was doing that kept me out all night, I told him the important thing was that whatever I was doing, which is not to say I was doing anything, was not going to interfere with my achieving the high goals he set for me in my last two years at school and we should get it behind us and move forward and then he **really**, like, lost it."

83

"O.K. We got a quorum."

"How is everything?"

"North American Day Trippers. They fly in every year about this time."

88

*"Excuse me, I hate to interrupt you. I just wanted to say
'nice weather we're having, isn't it'?"*

*"Next I'd like to read a love poem from my
pre-neutered romantic period."*

"It's getting ridiculous."

"The summer's over, Miss Harkavy. Let's see how you
manage on your own this winter and I'll see you
back here in Wellfleet next August."

"They're not born that way, Vern. They choose that life style. Believe me, a little therapy and they'd be dogs again."

94

"By the way, how's your brother?"

*"...so bless Mom and Dad and my little sister Kim
and I'll get back to you tomorrow night."*

98

"These West Coast people are beginning
to worry me."

"How come diamonds are a girl's best friend...
and a dog is man's?"

The A&P predicts its new self checkout
system will be a big hit with seniors.

"Last call!"

"I don't know, Kevin. I like you, too.
I just don't want to jeopardize my
heterosexual merit badge."

"Put your shirt on, Frank."

"Kowalsky... your table is ready."

*"Hello, you have reached your mother. If you want to talk
nice press one, if you want to fight press two,
if you want to complain press three, and
if you want to apologize I'm listening."*

"It says 'eat immediately'."

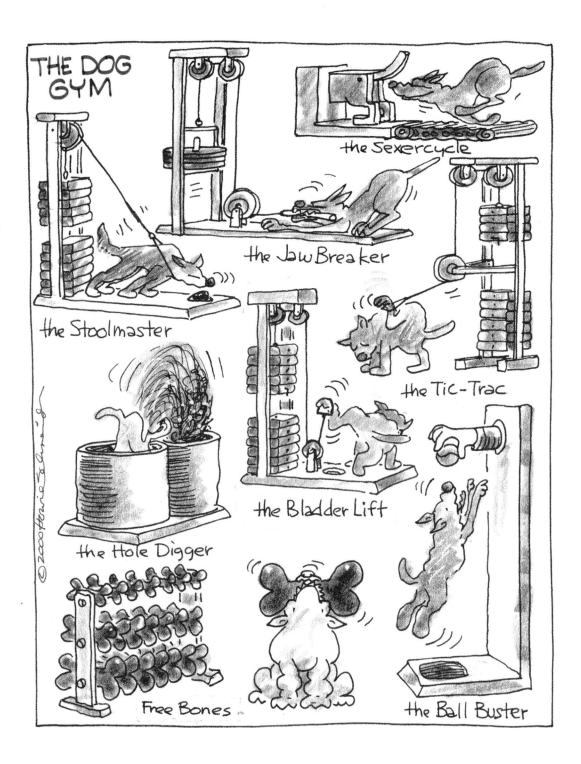

"My wife understands me."

"...and our special all this month is the restaurant itself. It comes with four rental units, fifty feet of beach front and an owner's apartment for just three million five, tonight's meal included."

*"Don't anybody move. Just put the keys to
a two-bedroom yearround rental in an envelope
and no one will get hurt."*

"God, I hate February."

"There definitely was a break-in, Chief, but as far as we can make out all they got were some dog bisquits."

"I may be way off-base here but it seems to me you're not considering the adaptability of your forms to their organic variations, and you're doing nothing to clarify your color blocks on the picture plane in relation to their contiguity or separation. But like I say, what the hell do I know?"

117

"Keep up the good work, Mr. Forbush."

"LIVE! LIVE! Cursed whale!"

*"Y'know what, Martha? I'm just going to lie here
and let Condoleeza handle everything."*

Kaht Yoga

the CROISSANT

the RISING SUN

the STUPID DOG

the CIRCLE of LIFE

the PLOW

the BOAT

the ICON

the HORSE SHOE CRAB

the TREE

the WOMAN

121

122

"Do you have any straight coffee... I mean 'plain' coffee?"

"Étude, Bruté?"

DOGGAIR, the airline of man's best friend

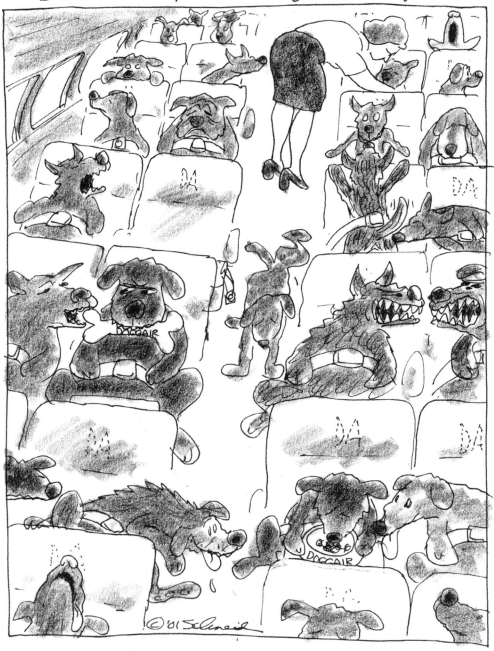

"I'll tell you what bugs me. I'm getting damn sick and tired of people asking me how the better half is doing."